Thumb Position School for Cello

by cassia harvey

CHP261

©2015 by C. Harvey Publications All Rights Reserved.

www.charveypublications.com - print books
www.learnstrings.com - PDF downloadable books
www.harveystringarrangements.com - chamber music

Note Charts

Bass Clef, Tenor Clef, and Treble Clef

Cassia Harvey

Bass Clef, Tenor Clef, and Treble Clef in Thumb Position

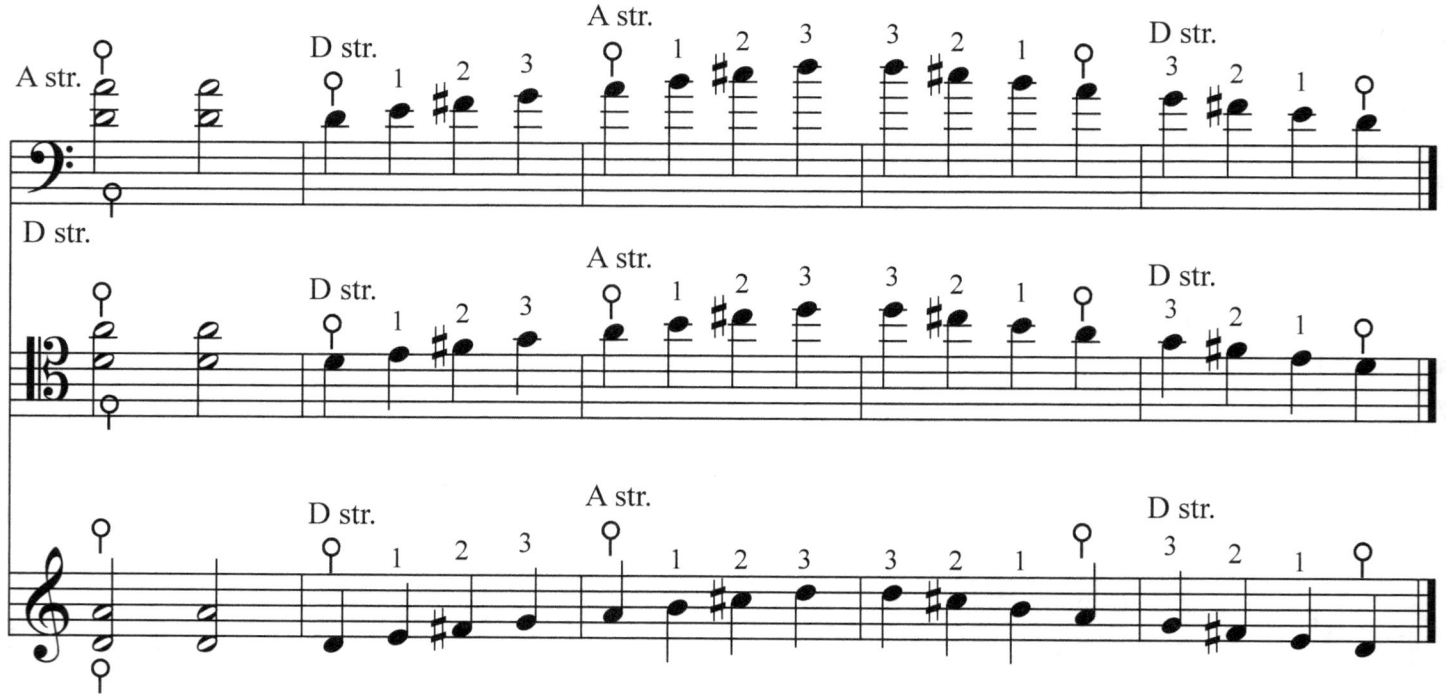

©2015 C. Harvey Publications All Rights Reserved.

Thumb Position School for Cello

Thumb Position

1. Place the thumb on its side, across two strings (start with the A and D strings). Play on the tips of the remaining fingers.

3. Keep the left wrist straight to support the hand and the thumb.

4. Press the string down completely with the thumb to build strength. The side of the knuckle (where the thumb bends) should be pressing the A string down. Depending on the length of your thumb, the side of the nail will be pressing the D string down. Later on, your hand will be on different sets of strings (D and G or G and C) however, the side of the knuckle is the strongest part of the thumb and should always be pressing down on one of the strings.

5. Balance over all the fingers and the thumb equally.

6. Building a thumb callus takes time. Start gradually and work up to playing more thumb position each day.

7. This is the sign for the thumb: ♀

Placing the Thumb

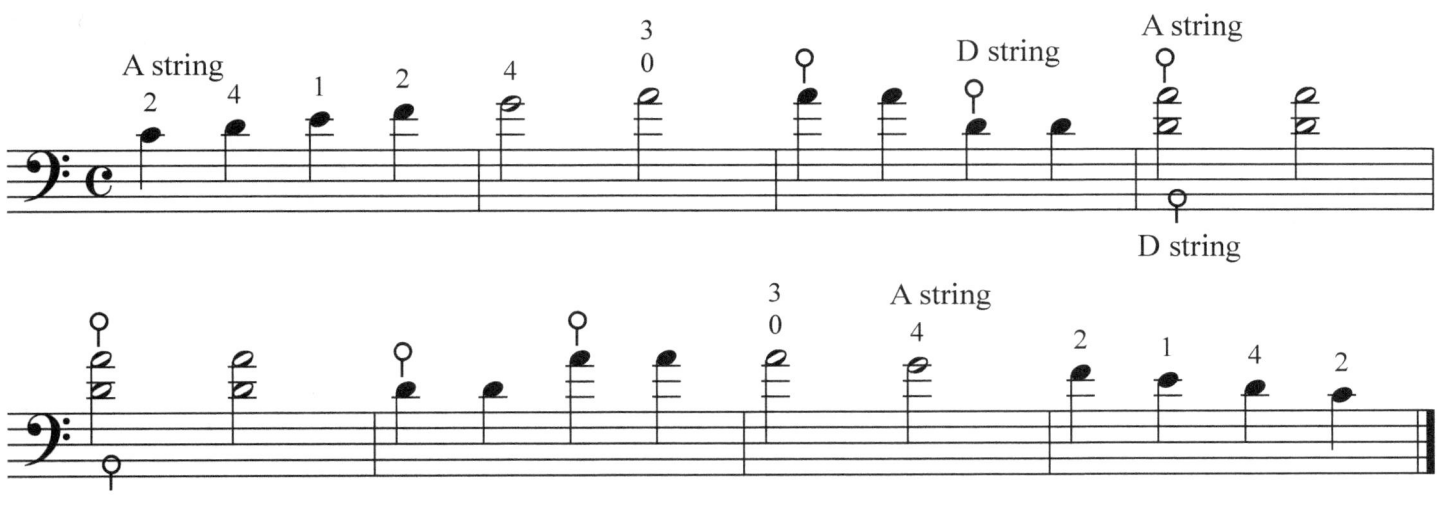

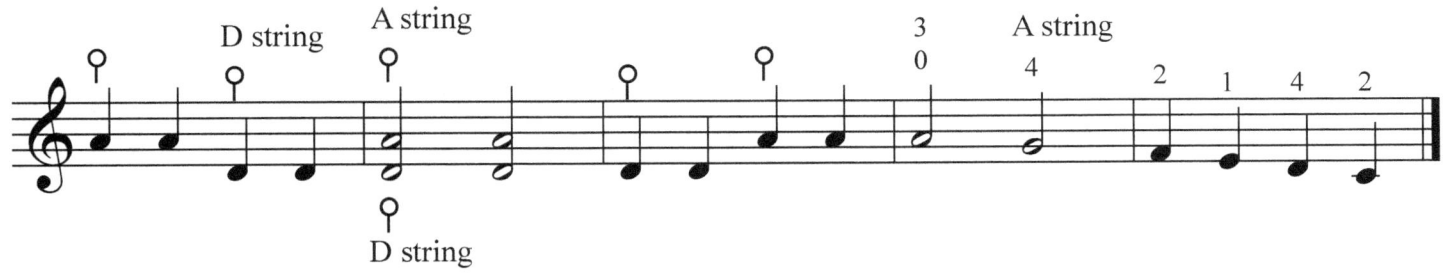

©2015 C. Harvey Publications All Rights Reserved.

Thumb Position with High 2nd Finger

Cassia Harvey

Intonation Study

Finger Exercise

©2015 C. Harvey Publications All Rights Reserved.

Third Finger

D Major Finger Exercise

Old Tune

Trad., arr. Harvey

The Gallant Ship

Trad., arr. Harvey

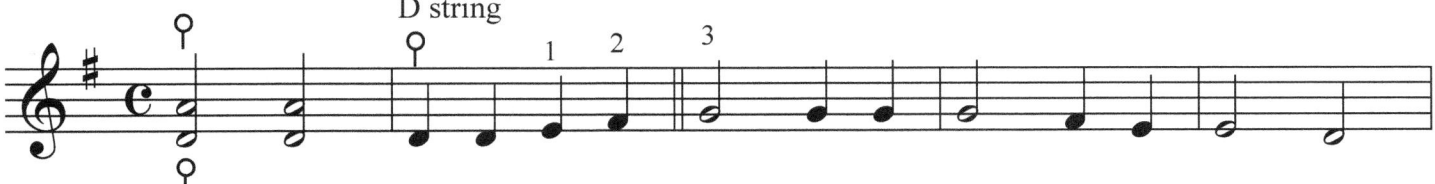
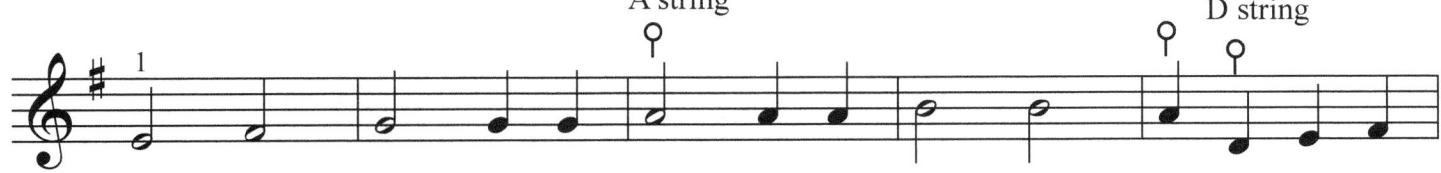

©2015 C. Harvey Publications All Rights Reserved.

Crossing Strings to 3rd Finger

D Major Scale Patterns

Shifting with the Thumb

The Little Pig

Trad., arr. Harvey

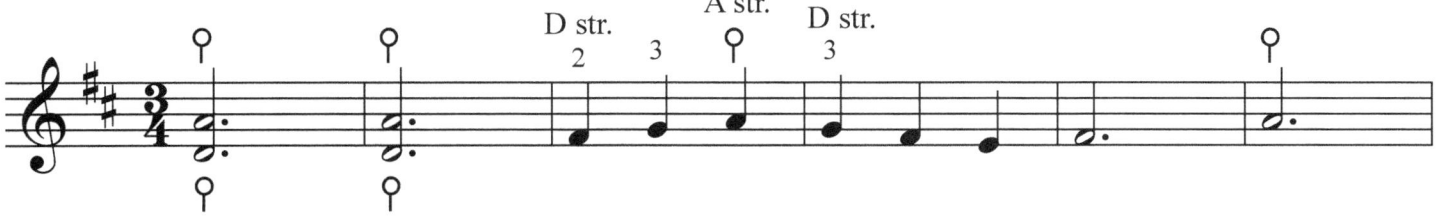

March Fragment

Handel, arr. Harvey

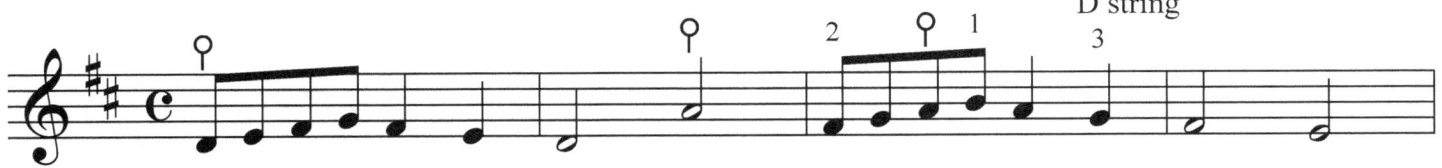

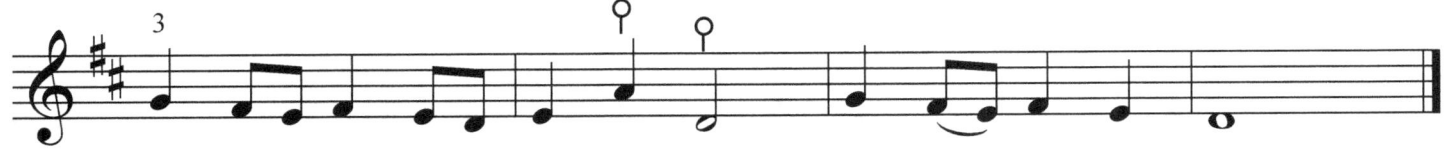

Thumb Position School for Cello

Shifting with the Thumb

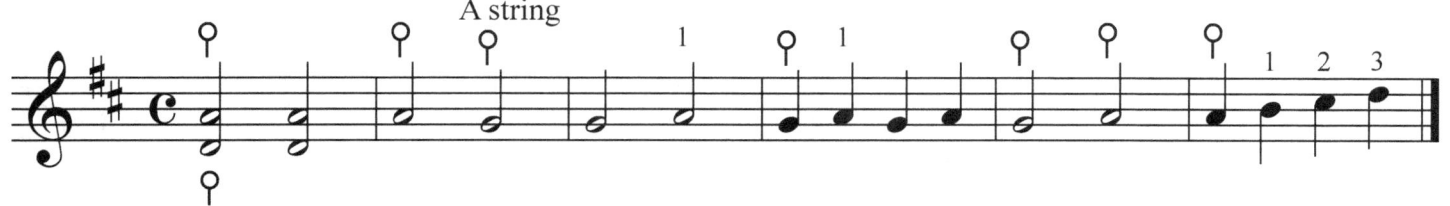

The Cat and the Fiddle

Trad., arr. Harvey

Lavender's Blue

Trad., arr. Harvey

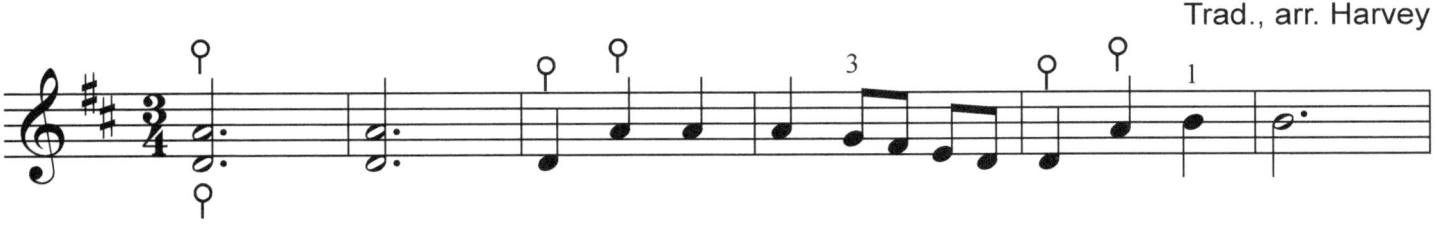

©2015 C. Harvey Publications All Rights Reserved.

Broken Thirds in D Major

D Major Skipping Study

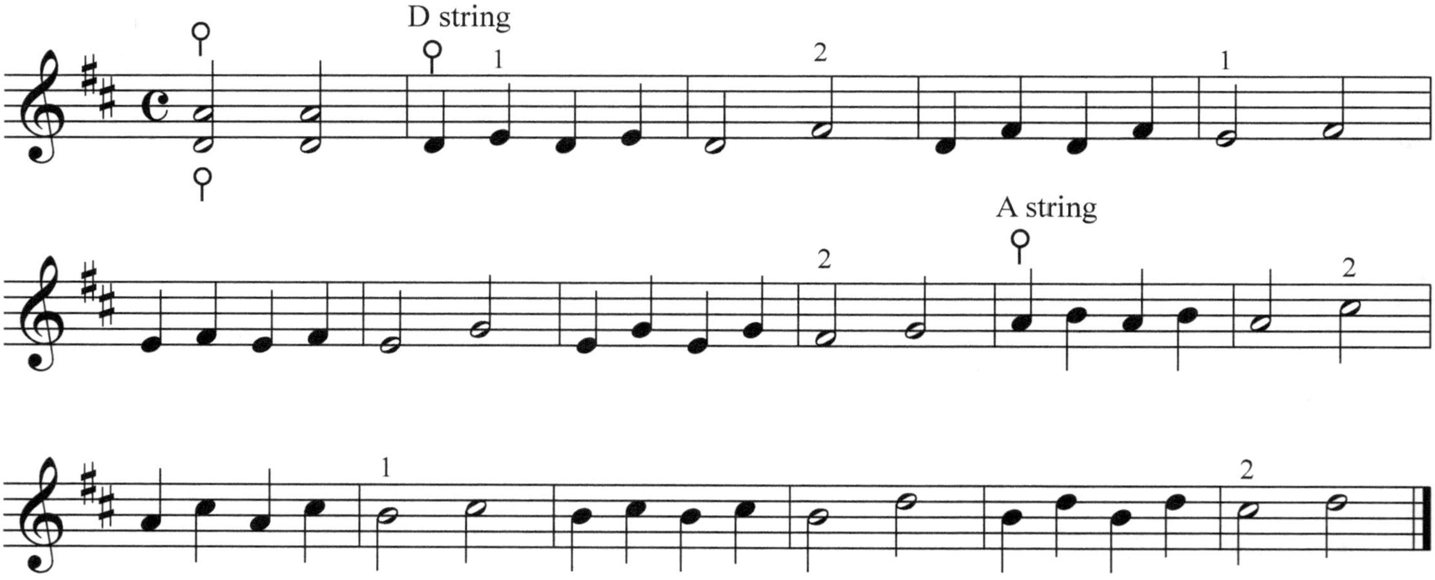

Shifting with the Thumb

D Major Skipping Patterns

D Major Study No. 5

Thumb Position School for Cello

Shifting with the Thumb

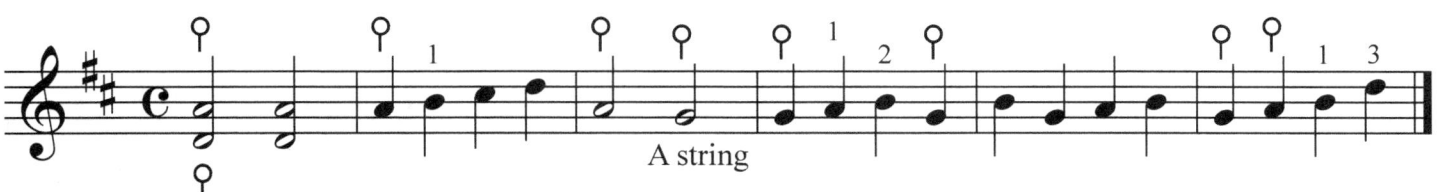
A string

Jasmine Flower

Trad., arr. Harvey

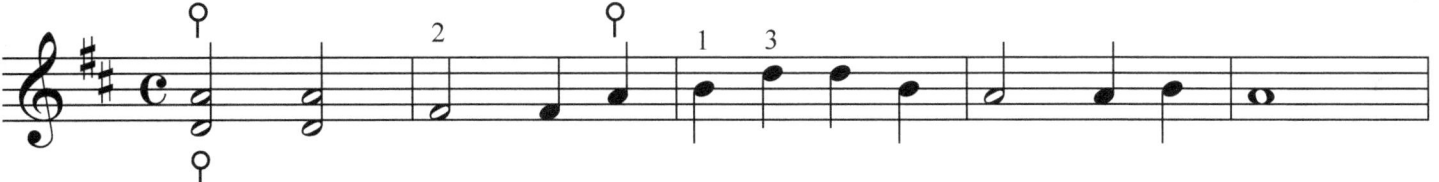

The Little Walnut Tree

Trad., arr. Harvey

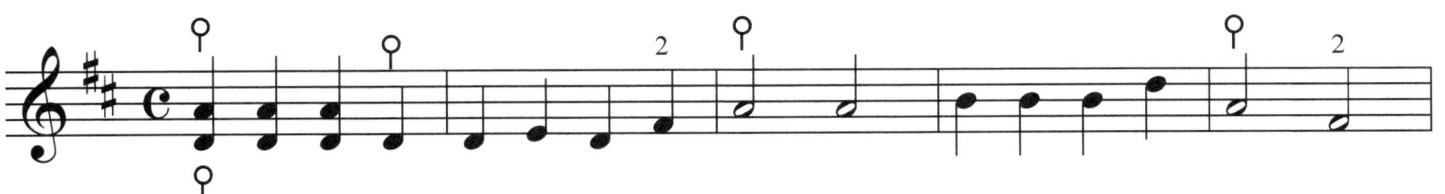

©2015 C. Harvey Publications All Rights Reserved.

D Major Broken Thirds

Broken Thirds Patterns

Under the Spreading Chestnut Tree

Trad., arr. Harvey

The Sandman Comes

Trad., arr. Harvey

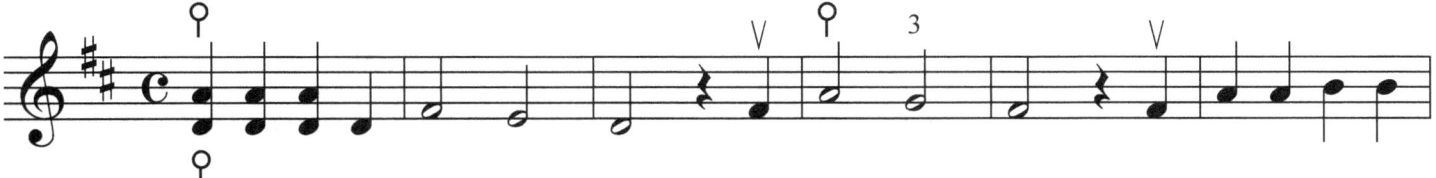

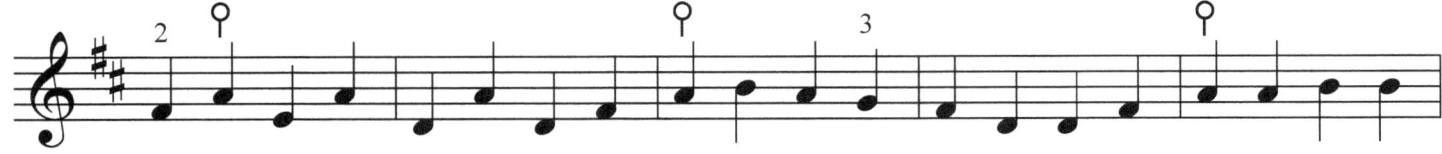

D Major Broken Fourths

Patterns with Fourths

D Major Octaves

Shifting with the Thumb

More Broken Intervals

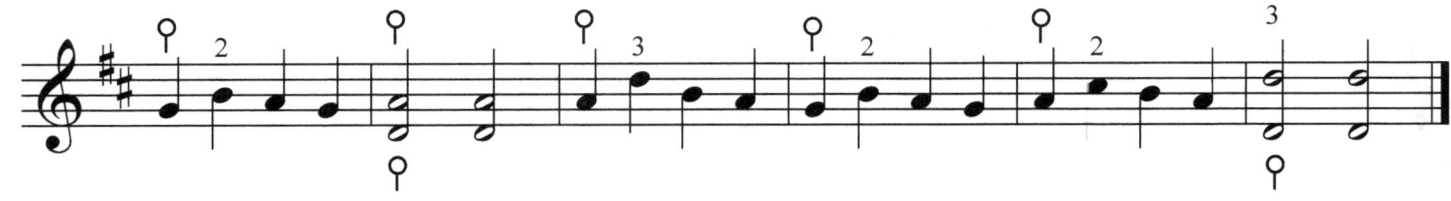

Tenor Clef on the A String

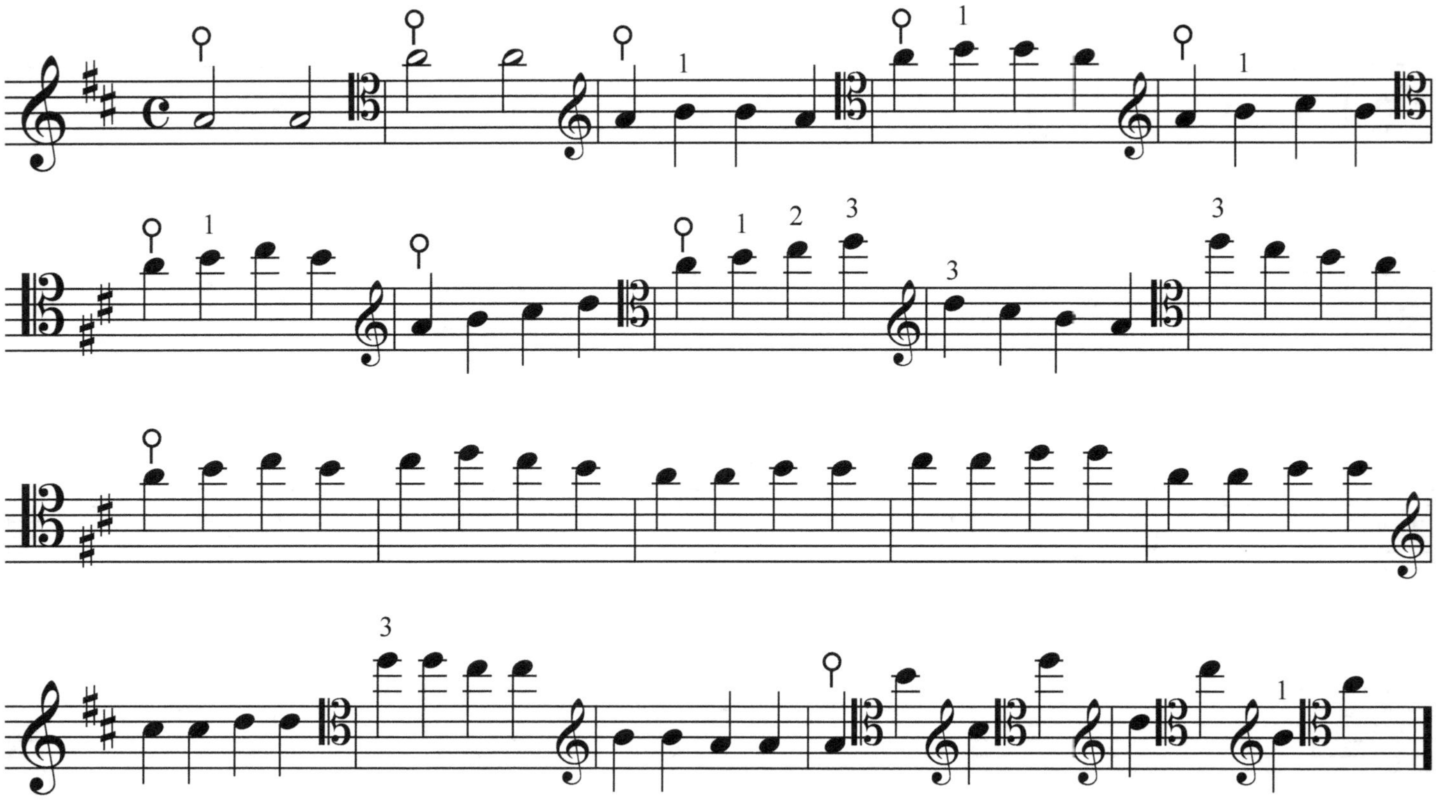

Tenor Clef on the A and D Strings

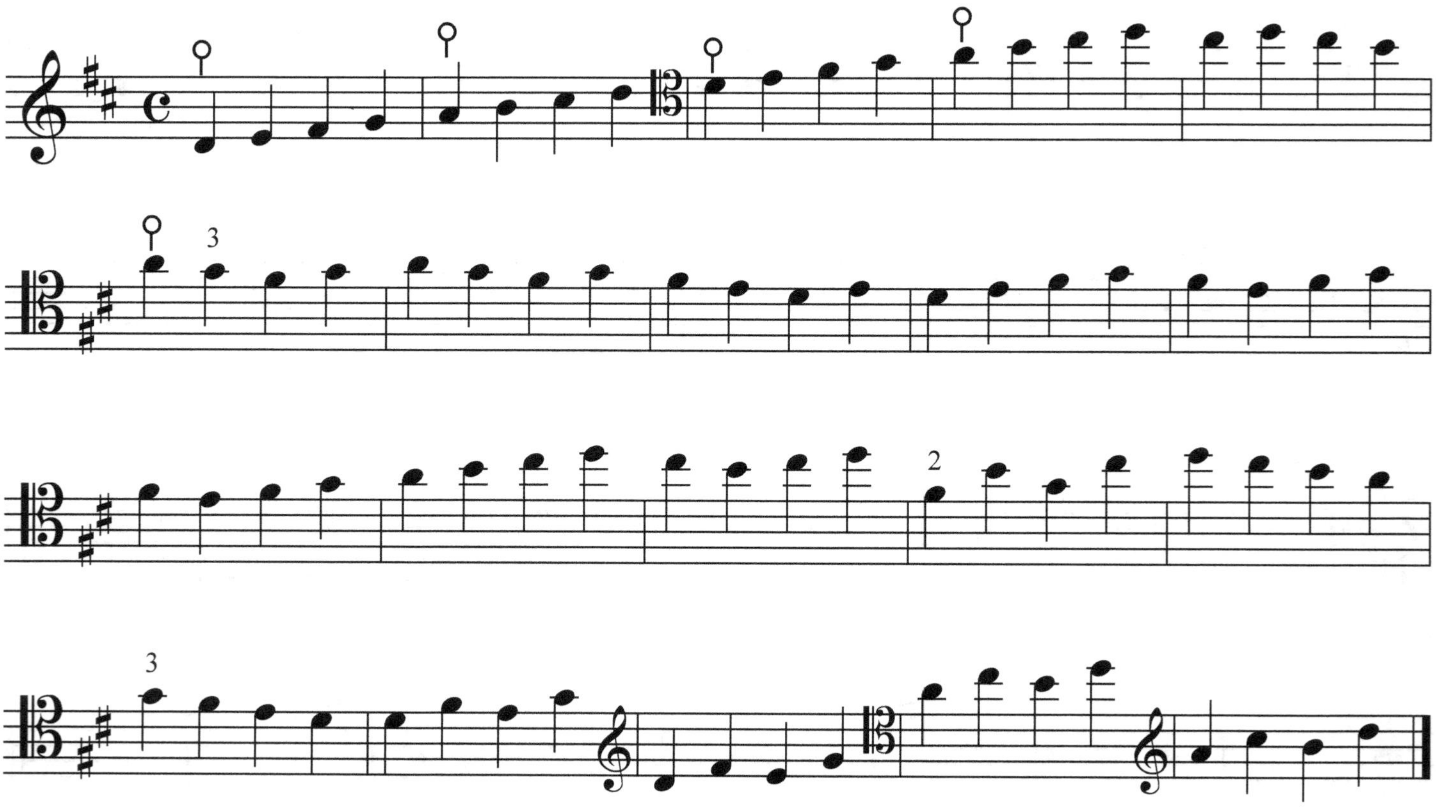

Thumb Position School for Cello

For more work in D major, pages focusing on extended 3rd finger can be found starting on page 72. Extended 3rd finger is used in the Duport and Vandini Sonatas.

Song of Dedication

Trad., arr. Harvey

From the Old Days

Trad., arr. Harvey

©2015 C. Harvey Publications All Rights Reserved.

Thumb Position with Low 2nd Finger

Low 2nd Finger Patterns

Thumb Position School for Cello

Hush, Little Baby
Trad., arr. Harvey

Mi Chacra
Trad., arr. Harvey

Low 2nd Finger Study

Low 2nd Finger Patterns

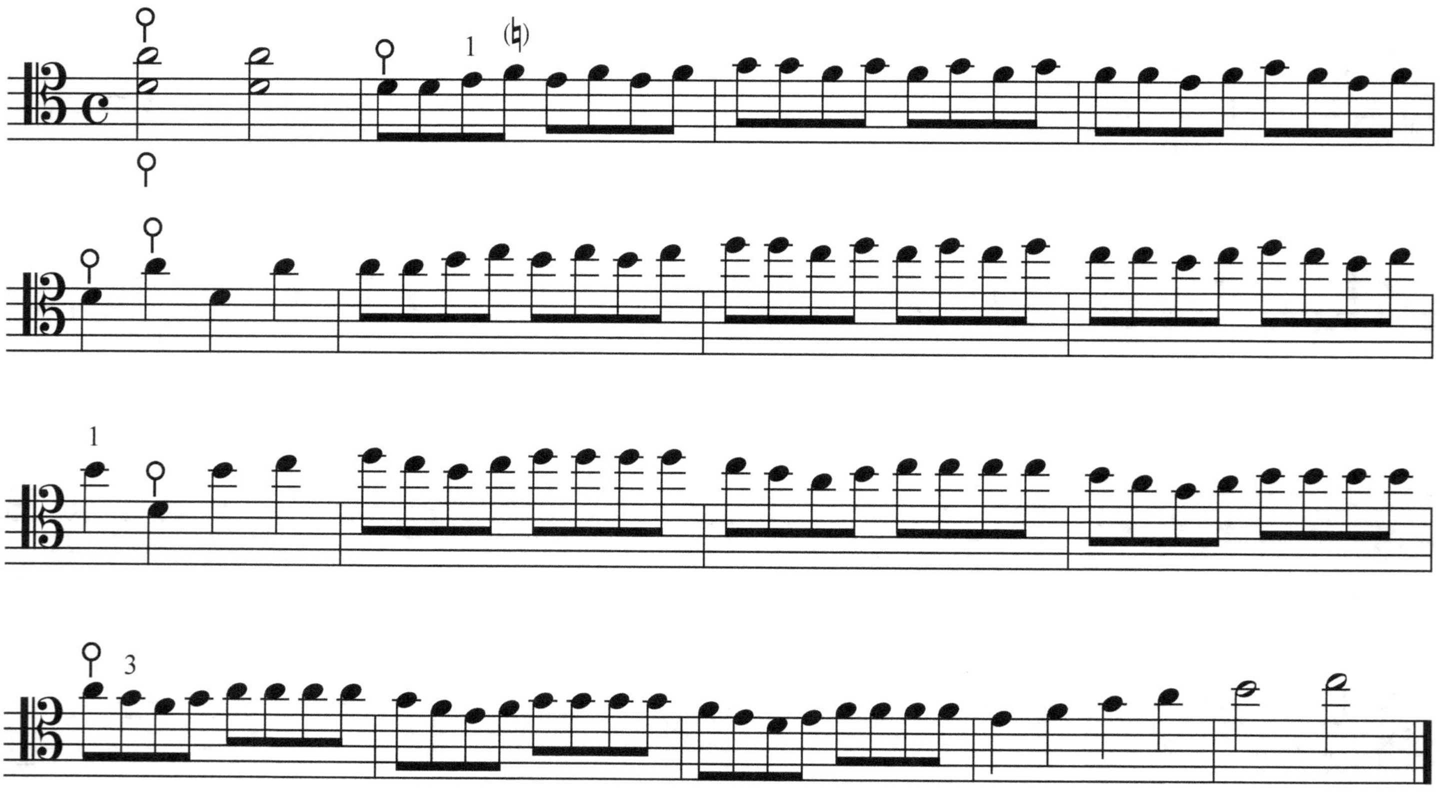

The Merry Widow Waltz

Lehar, arr. Harvey

Russian Children's Song

Trad., arr. Harvey

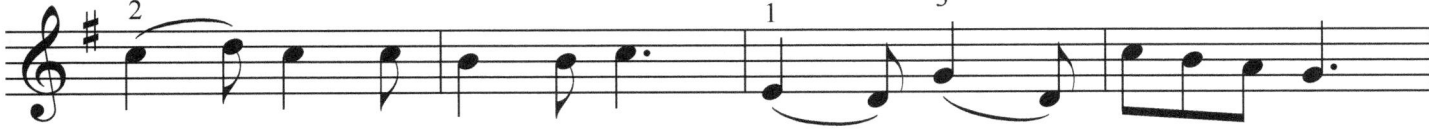

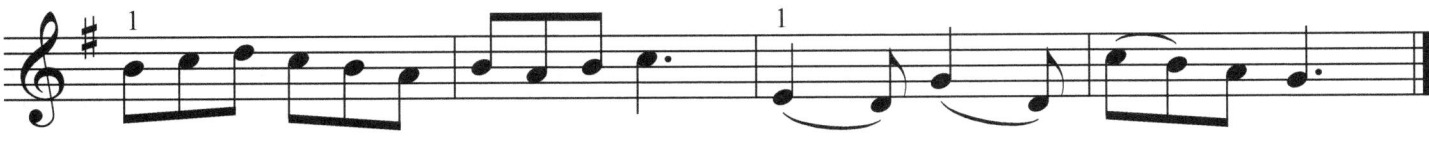

Skipping Notes With Low 2nd Finger

More Skipping

Thumb Position School for Cello

Shifting with the Thumb

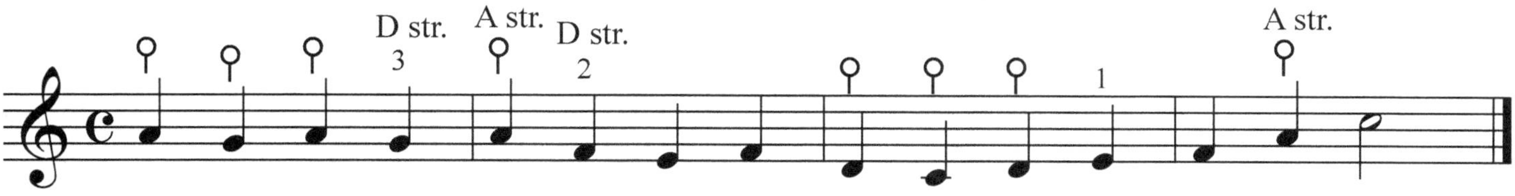

March
Harvey

Nine Hundred Miles
Trad., arr. Harvey

©2015 C. Harvey Publications All Rights Reserved.

3rd Finger C on the G String

C Major Study No. 1

Erie Canal

Trad., arr. Harvey

Song of the Castanets

Trad., arr. Harvey

C Major Study No. 2

Little Arpeggios

C Major Study No. 3

C Major Study No. 4

Marchioness of Huntsley

Marshall, arr. Harvey

High and Low 2nd Finger

Moving 2nd Finger Around

©2015 C. Harvey Publications All Rights Reserved.

Miss Platoff's Wedding

Gow, arr. Harvey

C♮ and F♯

More C♮ and F♯

Thumb Position School for Cello

The Little Pigeon

Trad., arr. Harvey

Sur le Pont D'Avignon

Trad., arr. Harvey

Thumb Position in G Major

G Major Study

C♮ and F♯ in G Major

Thumb Position School for Cello

Shifting With the Thumb

Moll Tierny

Trad., arr. Harvey

G Major Study in 6/8

G Major Arpeggio Study

German Waltz

Trad., arr. Harvey

The Notes on the G String

Across Strings in G Major

G Major Study

G String Patterns

Stretching Back to B♭ (Low First Finger)

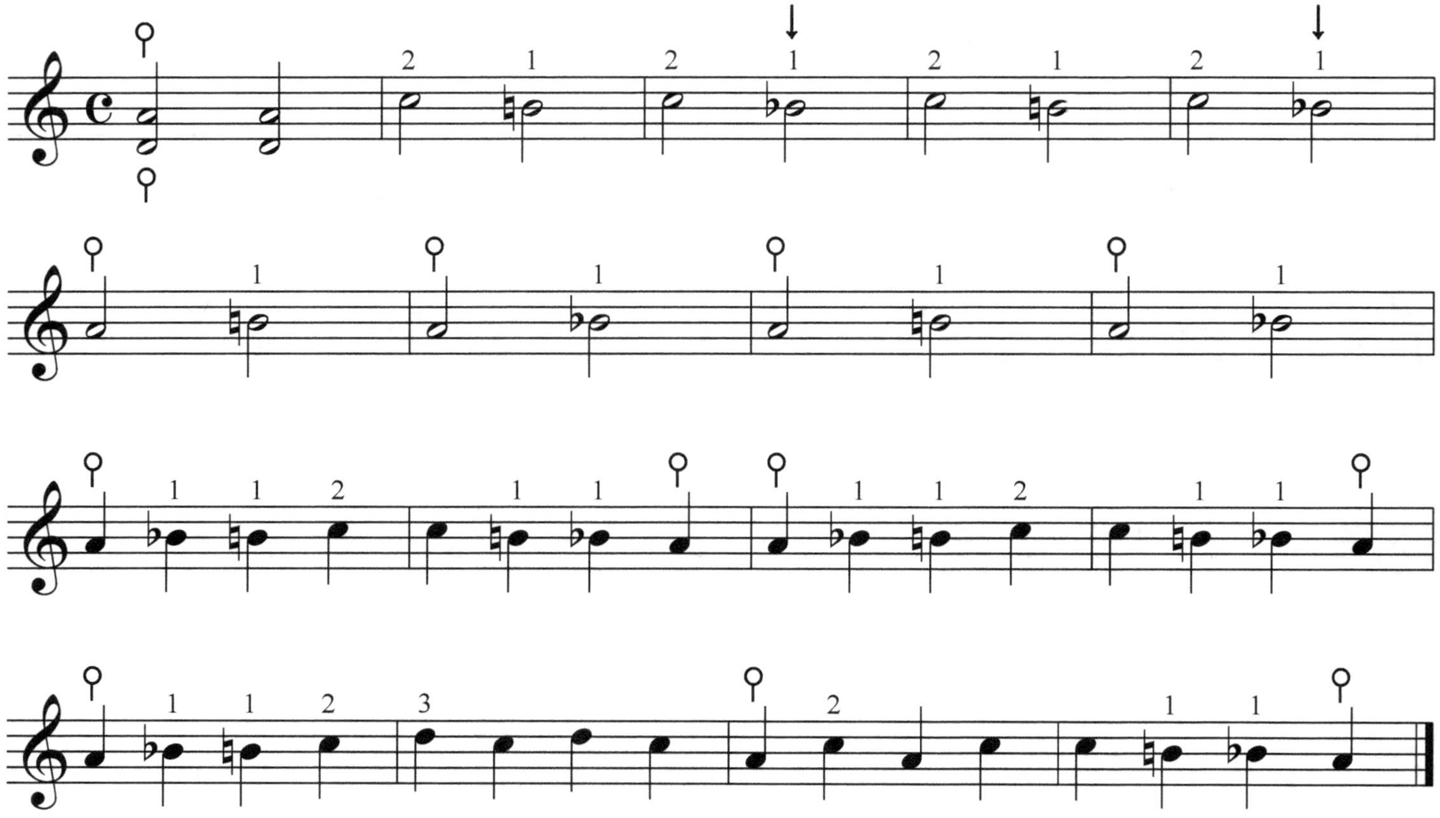

Low First Finger Study No. 1

Low First Finger Study No. 2

Low First Finger Study No. 3

London Hill

Trad., arr. Harvey

Low 2nd Finger: B♭ on the G String

Aragonaise

Massenet, arr. Harvey

©2015 C. Harvey Publications All Rights Reserved.

F Major Study No. 1

Shifting on Different Fingers

Rigaudon

Rameau, arr. Harvey

Love, Soft Illusion

Bertoni, arr. Harvey

The Odd Fellow's March

Trad., arr. Harvey

Skipping Notes in F Major

F Major Broken Thirds

Sonata

Marcello, arr. Harvey

Melody from 'The Mask of Comus'

Arne, arr. Harvey

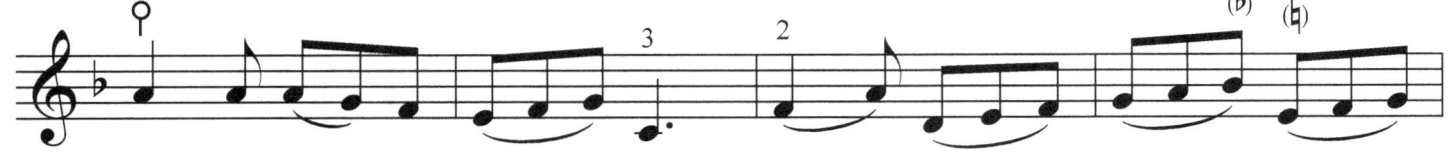

©2015 C. Harvey Publications All Rights Reserved.

Thumb Position School for Cello

Dissidence
Harvey

Accord
Harvey

In the Forest

Trad., arr. Harvey

Song of the Turkey

Findley, arr. Harvey

B♭ Study No. 2

(still on D string)

The Maid's Song

Johnson, arr. Harvey

B♭ Study No. 5

B♭ Study No. 6

A Mock Address to the French King

Corbett, arr. Harvey

Stretching to High 3rd Finger on the G String

Reaching Across to C#

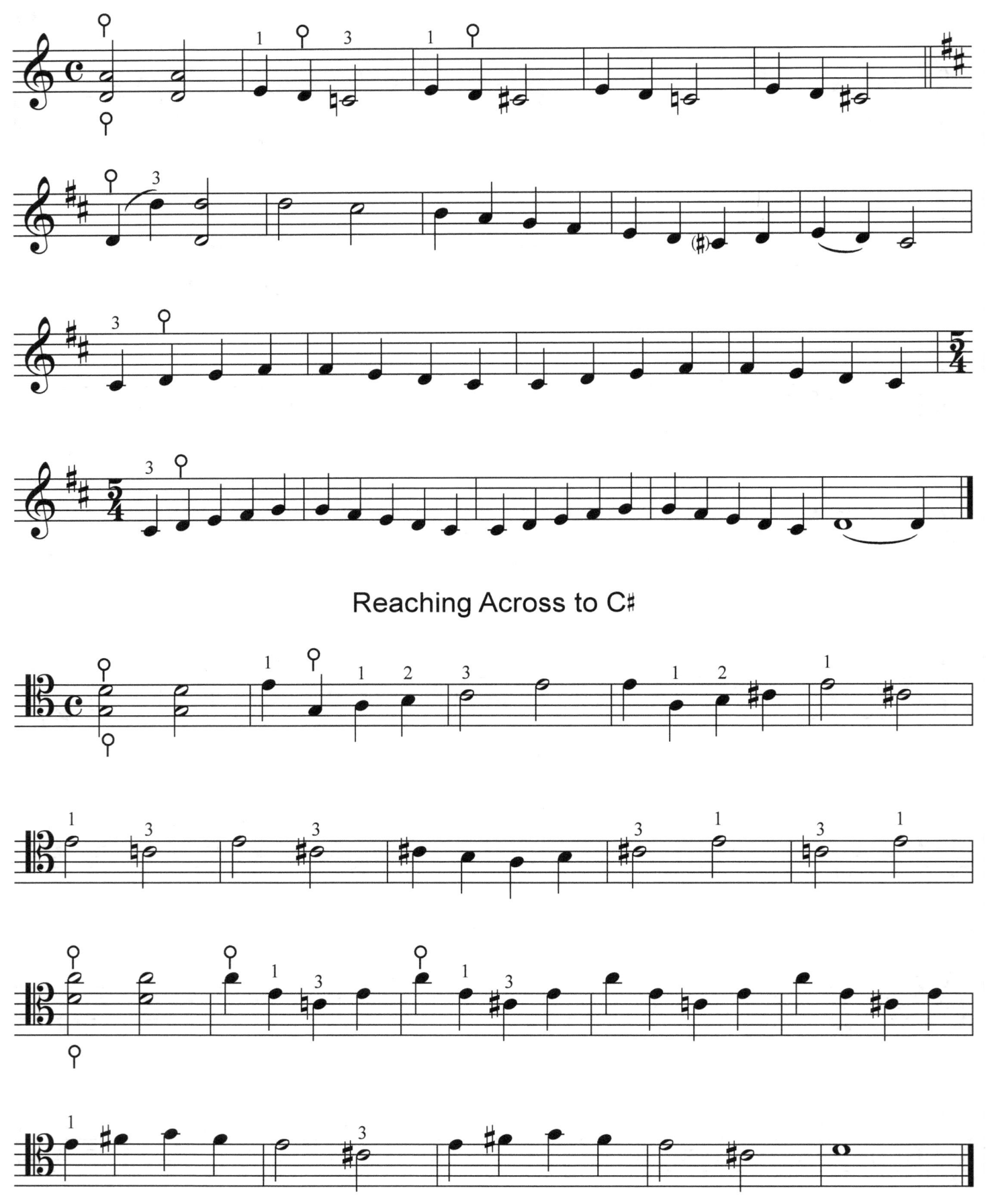

Thumb Position School for Cello

The Buds of May
Trad., arr. Harvey

The Fairy Dance
Trad., arr. Harvey

D Major Study No. 6

D Major Study No. 7

The Spanish Patriots

Trad., arr. Harvey

Vivace

Raoul, arr. Harvey

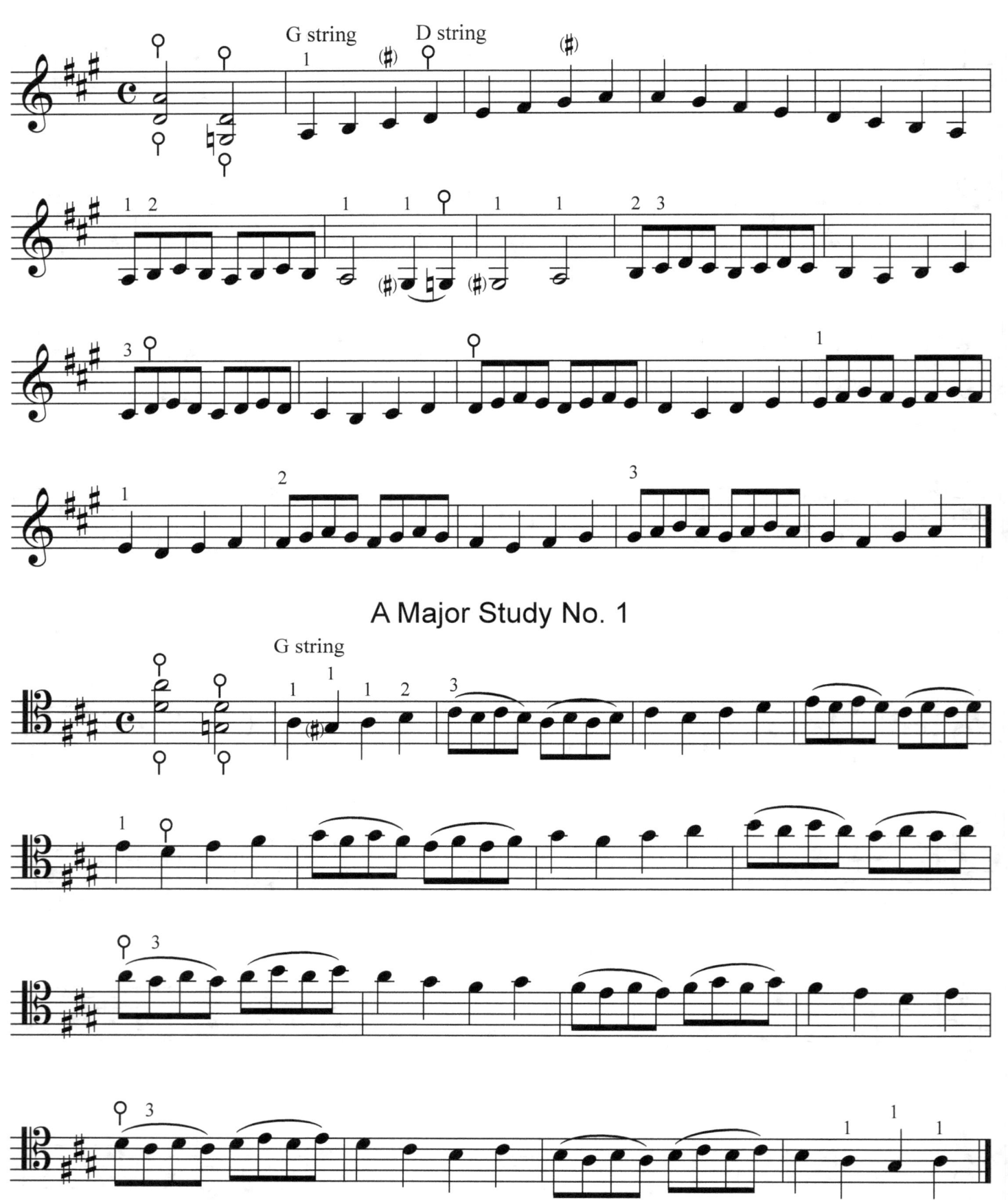

There Came to My Window...

Trad., arr. Harvey

French Folk Song and Variation

Trad., arr. Harvey

A Major Study No. 4

A Major Study No. 5

Hodgart's Delight

Trad., arr. Harvey

The Chapter of Fashions

Trad., arr. Harvey

A Major Study No. 6

A Major Study No. 7

Rondeau

Anon., arr. Harvey

A Few Scales

Also available from www.charveypublications.com: CHP356
Learning Three-Octave Scales on the Cello

Part One: Learning the Major Scales

C Major Scale

Cassia Harvey

©2019 C. Harvey Publications All Rights Reserved.

www.ingramcontent.com/pod-product-compliance
Lightning Source LLC
Chambersburg PA
CBHW051421070526

44584CB00023B/3527